THE CRAB MENTALITY DISEASE

How to Identify and Overcome Crab Mentality Disease & Virus in Yourself or Others

WANDA CURRIE

Dedication

This book is dedicated to the Survivors of
The Crab Mentality Disease
"From Generation to Generation,
IT ENDS WITH ME"

Contents

Introduction

Growing up, I could always see and feel that there was something wrong with how my family related, or should I say not relate to each other. As I became older, I learned that my family, like many families, was dysfunctional. Although there are many reasons family members don't function the way they should, I could easily see that they were extremely jealous and competitive toward each other. It was more like a war zone instead of a family. This behavior was played out through what I am calling The Crab Mentality Disease. Although my family started at the bottom of the barrel, the backwoods of North Carolina, where there always seemed like there was always strife, which was hidden behind closed doors. As a child, I would say that my family was cursed or bad blood. The light-skinned v dark-skinned, the educated v the uneducated, the haves v the haves not; the competition is endless. I have witnessed The Crab Mentality Disease destroy my family to the point of near extinction. I have never met or know most of my family. We never had family reunions or celebrated milestones: births, graduations, funerals, etc.

In 2017, as part of my personal healing journey and to learn more about my family history, I returned to North

Carolina for homecoming. While I was there, I visited the people I remember from the Annual Homecoming trips as a child. I honored my ancestors by visiting the Family Cemetery, attended the wedding of a cousin I had never met, took notes, got phone numbers, and asked lots of questions. There is a saying that you are as sick as your secrets. My family has been infected and affected by Crab Mentality Virus and disease for generations. When you heal yourself, you heal others from generation to generation. It ends with me!

Since then, I have continued to stay in contact with lost cousins and look forward to finding other lost family members as I continue to heal from The Crab Mentality Disease.

I grew up in Maryland and I love seafood. Maryland has the best crabs in the world. I enjoy eating steamed crabs. They are very good, but the human crabs are very bad.

The Crab Mentality Disease (CMD) is presented as a Spiritual Disease that is transmitted by the Crab Mentality Virus (CMV) from one human to another. When infected with the virus, it develops into The Crab Mentality Disease with symptoms that cause humans to act like crabs. This book is about HUMAN CRABS.

In this book, you will learn about The Crab Mentality Disease and Virus, what it is, and how it is transmitted. At the end of each chapter, there are spiritual and other interventions that have been used by me and others to overcome and be victorious over this deadly disease. There is help. You are not alone! These interventions work whether you are the person infected with Crab Mentality Disease (Human Crab), if you're affected by it as the target, or you're the Crab who wants to get out of the bucket and stay out the bottom of the barrel.

Due to the lasting trauma that is a part of being infected and affected by The Crab Mentality Disease, I did not include any of my personal stories. Instead, I have included some of the healing tools I use daily. Also, there are spaces in the book to write your healing and restoration story.

WHAT IS CRAB MENTALITY DISEASE?

"If I can't have it, neither can you"

Crab Mentality is an attitude where people react negatively in words, thoughts, and actions toward those who get ahead of them even though it does not appear to be beneficial

Crabs, in a bucket behavior, were first noticed by crab fishers. After they finished catching crabs and putting them in buckets, the fisherman saw the following:

It would start when one of the crabs would try to escape.

When the other crabs saw one crab trying to get out of the bucket, the other crabs were pulling the crab back down into the bucket.

This behavior was repeated every time a crab tried to get out of the bucket. The group of crabs at the bottom would stop it from leaving them.

Because of this behavior, the fisherman didn't have to put a lid on the bucket; they knew that every time one crab tries to get out of the bucket, the other crabs would pull it back down to the bottom.

People infected with Crab Mentality Disease (CMD) caused by Crab Mentality Virus (CMV) treat and interact with people just like the crabs in a bucket. They are Human Crabs that work together to prevent the success of an individual.

The major difference between human crabs and crabs that are meant for eating is that when raw crabs do it, it's their natural behavior and no purpose is attached to it.

On the other hand, human crabs are often motivated by jealousy, envy, lack of identity, misplaced loyalty, and other reasons. Their mindset is motivated by the thought: *"If I can't have it, neither can you."*

The Crab Mentality Disease is deep-rooted and destructive. It is not just about stopping people from making progress physically; it is an intentional plan that targets a person mentally, physically, and spiritually. It is passed from person to person and steals, kills, and destroys individuals, families, and communities.

People infected with the Crab Mentality Virus will often try to break the spirit of others, attacking their self-confidence and making them believe they're not good enough to break free from the bucket to pursue the destiny that they were created for.

But what's tragic about Crab Mentality Disease is everybody loses. When people try to hurt each other, it eventually results in the group, family, or organization's failure.

Here are two newer definitions from the Urban Dictionary:

Crab Mentality—a person who does not want another person to succeed by showing the following actions: disloyalty, jealousy, slander, two-faced behavior.

Crab in a Bucket—used to describe a person (or subculture) that does everything in his/her power to destroy the ambitions of those among them who wish to improve themselves.

Crab Mentality Disease Around the World

The Crab Mentality Virus is everywhere. Here are some other examples of how The Crab Mentality Disease infects and affects others.

There is a story from outside the US about long spoons and a group of people. They are seated at a table with food that they couldn't eat because the spoons they have are too long for them to feed themselves. The story ends with everyone not eating and staying hungry.

The point of the story is that people should have used long spoons to feed each other. So, showing how helping and supporting other people in certain instances is very important and can benefit everyone.

Schadenfreude is a German word that is defined as a person who feels pleasure, joy, or happiness from finding out about or seeing the troubles, failures, or humiliation of other people. This is mostly directed at people with whom they have a relationship with family, friends or co-workers. Since they have regular contact with the person, they are the first to know when something bad happens to them.

Herd Mentality — sometimes referred to as gang or pack mentality — describes how people are taught by other people and the culture to support and behave negatively. It is solely based on emotions and feelings instead of truth. Gang Mentality causes people to get along, making decisions that they would not make if they were not afraid of the consequences of making a choice different from everyone else.

The Dog in the Manger is a story about envy and selfishness, a person who keeps something that they do not need or want out of spite, deliberately causing hurt by keeping someone else from getting it. This is sometimes known as Misery Loves Company or Hurt people, Hurt people.

In Australia and New Zealand, The Tall Poppy Syndrome is a combination of opinions, emotions, and behaviors. It is when individuals or groups hold back, criticize and sabotage people who have been successful mostly in obtaining education and moving out of poverty. "Cutting down the tall poppy" is a description of the actions done on purpose to others who are tall from having goals, working hard, and achieving them.

In Japan, the expression "the nail that sticks up gets hammered down" means stay down, or you will end up being the target that will be beaten back down by the rest of the crabs to where you belong.

In the Netherlands, there is a saying "don't put your head above ground" so just stay down, do not rise and shine

The Bible, John 10:10: the thief comes only to steal, kill and destroy…

My Healing Journey

1. What Happened to you?

2. How do I feel about this?

3. What Impact is The Crab Mentality Disease having on you

4. What can you learn from your past?

5. What do you need to let go of?

Scripture

Jesus saw him lying there and knew the man had been sick a long time. Jesus said to him, "Would you like to be healed?" John 5:6 NLT.

Prayer

Father, thank you for this day. One of your names is Jehovah Rapha, the lord God that heals (Exodus 15:26). I believe and trust you. I have Faith and will do the work. Thank you for trained helpers. Thank you for divine intervention. You said that you will give me the desires of my heart. I want to be whole in my body, in my mind and in my heart. I declare I am healed, Amen.

Music is Medicine

From Wanda's Playlist:

Balm in Gilead — Richard Smallwood

Set The Atmosphere—Kurt Carr

Find Your Song

LET THE HEALING BEGIN!

CHAPTER 2

WHAT CAUSES CRAB MENTALITY DISEASE?

The Greatest Enemy to Success is Fear

The root cause of The Crab Mentality Disease is Fear.

What is Fear? A basic definition of fear is a powerful emotion caused by the belief that someone or something is dangerous, likely to cause pain or a threat. Since we want to stop the spread of this sickness, let's add this definition F.E.A.R. Face Everything And Recover.

There are 5 major fears connected with the Crab Mentality Virus:

1. Fear of failure. Some people are so afraid that if they try to do anything different, they will fail, causing them to feel embarrassment and shame. They fear other people will know that they failed and laugh at

them. That is why they have learned to accept and like being at the bottom, because it's safe and comfortable.

2. Fear of rejection. Everyone has the need for love and acceptance, especially from their family and community. When a person is verbally bullied, "you think you are better than us" and is treated differently because they choose to live a more excellent way, it can cause them to go backward instead of forward. This reaction is often seen in poor communities infected with Crab Mentality Disease. Because of jealousy or self-hatred, its members will find and use anything to pull that person back down to the community's level.

3. Fear of success is that a person may stay infected and affected because they do not feel that they can handle the consequences of being successful. Sayings like "don't forget where you came from" or "don't forget your family, can reinforce a person's fear and stop them from removing themselves from what they know is an unhealthy environment. This could include attending college, moving, traveling, making new friends or pursuing activities in order to get out and stay out of the bottom of the pot.

4. Fear of the Unknown. If you are infected or affected by Crab Mentality Disease, then acting like a crab is all you have been exposed to. It is scary to change; it requires risk and letting go of people, places and things while changing. It can take anywhere from 21 to 90 days to develop healthy habits, and much of that process is spent not knowing the outcome.

5. Fear of Being Alone. Some may have heard the saying, "it's lonely at the top." There's a difference between

being alone and being lonely. Honestly, recovering from Crab Mentality Disease is painful. You will be lonely and alone while changing behaviors that are bloodline. Just remember it is worth it because freedom is not free.

These five distinct fears are the life of the Crab Mentality Virus & Disease. False Evidence Appearing Real is what prevents the infected crabs from wanting to leave the bottom of the barrel. The crabs stuck in the bottom are so afraid; they stop any crab from leaving because of their Fear.

My Healing Journey

1. What would you do if you were not afraid?

2. What would you do if you knew you couldn't fail?

3. What is the risk if you change?

4. If nothing changes, what will that cost you?

5. What's next?

Scripture

For God did not give us a spirit of timidity or cowardice or fear, but [He has given us a spirit] of power and of love and of sound judgment and personal discipline [abilities that result in a calm, well-balanced mind and self-control].
2 Timothy 1 AMP

Prayer

Lord thank you that I can come to you for safety and healing. In the name of Jesus, I renounce Fear and its fruits: depression, anxiety, anger, rejection and unforgiveness in my life. Fear will not have power over my thoughts, mind, and my heart. I declare I will not be moved by fear, I will move by Faith—In Jesus' Name — Amen

Music is Medicine

From Wanda's Playlist:

Fear is a Liar — Zach Williams

Brave - Sara Bareilles

Find Your Song

I WANT TO HEAL!

What Is Crab Mentality Virus?

We are not fighting against humans. We are fighting against forces and authorities and against rulers of darkness and powers in the spiritual world
Ephesians 6:12 (CEV)

Once a person is infected with the Crab Mentality Virus, and left untreated, it will become Crab Mentality Disease (CMD).

The Infection and transmission of the Crab Mentality Virus always starts with the family and community. The reason is that all crabs (human and the eating crabs) start out together in the same place — in a barrel, bucket or within a closed environment.

The Crab Mentality Virus is a highly contagious SPIRITUAL VIRUS. Once infected with the virus, it easily spreads from person to person, until it turns into Crab Mentality Disease. This illness causes the infected person to act like a crab. When that happens, they are human crabs infected and affected. The CMV spreads by the behaviors being repeated to whomever they interact with regularly.

The exact reason a person becomes infected with the Crab Mentality Virus is not known. Here are some reasons: viewing other people's progress as a threat, it was caught; it was taught, or it's a way someone thinks.

The Crab Mentality Virus is a mindset. The two mindsets are:

1. Growth Mindset

"Failure is an opportunity to Grow"

Here are the things you might hear from someone who wants to leave the barrel say:

I can learn to do anything I want. Challenges help me grow. My effort and attitude determine my success. Feedback is helpful. I am encouraged, inspired, and uplifted by the success of others. I like to try new things.

Using affirmations, prayers and other tools can help reach your goals while you are healing from The Crab Mentality Disease

2. Fixed Mindset

"Failure is the limit of my abilities"

Here are certain things you will hear from someone who is infected with the Crab Mentality Virus say:

I'm either good at it or I'm not. I can't learn to do new things. I can either do it or I can't. My future is already set. If something is too hard, I give up. I take all feedback as a personal criticism. I do what I know how to do.

If you say any or act out on these statements, you're more than likely to have Crab Mentality Disease and are a danger to yourself and others.

My healing Journey

1. Do I listen to what I tell myself?

2. What other choices do I have?

3. What do you need to say no to?

4. If nothing changes, what will it cost you?

5. What is one action you could take in the next 10 minutes?

Scripture

Be careful how you think, your life is shaped by your thoughts Proverbs 4:23 (GNT)

Prayer

Abba Father, thank you for this day. Thank you, that I can talk to you anytime I need to. I want to be transformed. I want my mind renewed (Romans 12:2) I want to be a new creation. In the name of Jesus, I break the bondage of a fixed mindset that is being used by Crab Mentality Virus and Disease against me, my family and anyone who is in connected to me. What is not transformed is transferred. From generations to generations, I'm ending it! In the Name that is above every name, Jesus Amen.

Music is Medicine

From Wanda's Playlist:

Recover – Jennifer Lewin

He Will Never Leave You – Alvin Darling & Celebration

Find Your Song

I CAN HEAL!

The Dangers of Crab Mentality

Nothing in this world is more dangerous than sincere ignorance and conscientious stupidity
— Dr. Martin Luther King, Jr

Crab Mentality Virus causes negative thinking and crab-like behaviors in the person infected with it. Without intervention, it will develop into The Crab Mentality Disease which is passed on to others.

The affected person is the target since the crab-like behavior is first directed toward the person trying to get out of the bucket. This disease is cunning, baffling, and powerful. It is on assignment to kill, steal and destroy. When someone has The Crab Mentality Disease, they can sometimes be the victim and at other times they may act like the other crabs.

Here is a list of other consequences of the Crab Mentality Virus (CMV)

1. CMV prevents notable achievement through sabotage from others. The affected person begins to self-sabotage and stops achieving to protect themselves from abuse.

2. CMV hinders the ability of individuals to learn how to resolve conflicts, since these families and groups only know how to compete and fight among themselves.

3. CMV creates a toxic environment for people infected and affected who are mostly in contact with sick

people. This provides a doorway for many other spiritual viruses such as greed, jealousy, and pride.

4. CMV causes people to waste time and energy focusing on other people's lives, instead of using it to develop themselves.

5. CMV causes people to act in a way that is socially undesirable to others due to fear of contamination. It pushes other people away, resulting in isolation.

The behavior is now normal due to prolonged exposure to human crabs. This isolation limits interaction with people who live a positive, progressive, and healthier lifestyle that can become a source of hope and inspiration.

My Healing Journey

1. How do you sabotage or harm yourself?

2. What do you really want?

3. What do I need to say yes to?

4. What will you do differently?

5. What can you change now?

Scripture

Indeed, we too were once stupid, disobedient, and misled. We were slaves to many kinds of lusts and pleasures. We were mean and jealous. We were hated, and we hated each other. Titus 3:3 (GWT)

Prayer

Lord, I cast down every proud thing that has been raised against your knowledge. (2 Corinthians 10:5) I was not created to think and act like a crab. I repent for and renounce acting like a crab. I was created for good works.

Develop in me your fruit: love, joy, peace, long-suffering, gentleness, goodness, faith, meekness, and temperance. (Galatians 5:22) Faith without work is dead. I will not just pray about how I think and what I do, I will change the behaviors that I repented and renounced. When I fall short, I will forgive myself, forgive others, and continue my healing process. In Jesus Name, Amen.

Music is Medicine

From Wanda's Playlist:

Change Me – Tamela Mann

Never Lost – Tauren Wells

Find Your Song

HEALING IS FOR ME!

CHAPTER 3

JEALOUSY & ENVY

Anger is cruel and destructive, but it's nothing compared to jealousy
Proverbs 27:4 (GNT)

Jealousy and envy are emotions that we all feel from time to time. It's normal. When the feelings of envy and jealousy control someone's life, it changes how they think about everything.

It stops others from realizing dreams and goals, resulting in destructive and self-destructive behaviors.

While most people think jealousy and envy mean the same thing, they are different.

Envy is defined as a feeling of discontent and resentment caused by someone else's possessions or qualities that you want. Envy is towards things.

Jealousy is a feeling that has to do with feeling being threatened by someone else. When someone feels jealous, they are afraid of losing something. Jealousy is toward a person.

Some Causes of Envy & Jealousy

Envy is often rooted in **low self-esteem** that usually develops in early childhood from such negative experiences like:

- Emotionally distant parents.

- Sexual, physical, or emotional abuse.

- Academic difficulties.

- Social beauty standards.

Low self-esteem may cause a person to be envious in three major areas:

1. Taking Other People's Success Personally.
Low self-esteem causes depression and shame. When they see people that they intimately know achieve success, it triggers feeling about their current reality: "I should have what someone else has and since I don't have it, I look and feel bad." The reality is they really don't know how the person they are envious of became successful.

2. Selfish Ambition
Envy starts with desire. There's nothing wrong with the desire for material things as long as they are realistic and balanced, the opposite is GREED. There is also a need to recognize that there are more important things that money can't buy.

Selfish ambition is PRIDE. The person ends up elevating and putting themselves above everybody. They become ruthless and will betray family, friends, and enemies to get what they want.

3. Yearning for Status & Achievement

There is nothing wrong with wanting recognition for our achievements and to do your best to be the best. Yearning is defined as an intense longing for something. Overtime, it becomes a craving or a competitive spirit that will attempt to outdo everyone else.

When that happens, envy is at the root. We don't accept ourselves as we are. We do not recognize our talents and strengths, causing us to be envious of others.

Now that you know the destructive nature of envy, this is how someone who is envious may act toward you:

- Putting you down—either openly or undercover.

- Provoking a reaction in you, from anger to sadness to outrage—then standing back and getting off on your reactions.

- Undermining your opinion or voice so you start to doubt yourself.

- Using sarcasm—disguised as 'humor' — to make fun at your achievements, by mocking what you believe in.

- Copying you — or deceptive actions to prevent an important event from happening.

- Flattery—excessive and dishonest praise, given especially to further one's own interest.

Jealousy and Envy are dangerous feelings that can lead to:

Murder— literally wanting to get rid of the person so that you can get what they have. Evil thoughts that something bad will happen to them.

Strife— constant tensions between everyone, loves drama.

Greed — insatiable desire for money and material things, jealousy toward financially successful people.

Anger—this spirit is usually hidden and comes in outbursts toward the target of jealousy.

Division—the forming of a group (s) of other sick people as partners who will agree and justify their feelings so that they can gang up against the person they are envious of.

Slander—speaking half-truths or complete lies, character assassination and smear campaigns used to discredit and harm others.

Healing from Envy and Jealousy

The Crab Mentality Disease is bloodline related and is passed from generation to generation. As part of your healing journey, take a brief family history. Look at your brothers, sisters, parents, aunt, and uncles. Is there a pattern of family members being jealous/envious of other family members?

If you have identified jealousy or envy as a behavior that you have been infected or affected, you can change it! What is not transformed is transferred, what was learned can be unlearned. It won't be easy, but it's necessary. Here are some steps you can take to accomplish that.

1. Acknowledge that you are envious
2. Recognize that pride is just the other side of the envy.
3. Replace envy with inspiration
4. Let envy motivate self-improvement
5. Don't forget to be thankful for your gift, talents and blessings

My Healing Journey

1. Am I happy?

2. What's missing in my life?

3. What do I want?

4. Why do I want it?

5. Am I willing to work for it?

Scripture

So then let us not sleep [in spiritual indifference] as the rest [of the world does], but let us keep wide awake [alert and cautious] and let us be sober [self-controlled, calm, and wise]. 1 Thessalonians 5:6 AMP

Prayer

Thank you, Jesus, that I can come to you about anything. I know I am an envious person. Envy is a spiritual infection. It is wrong for me to want what others have when it doesn't belong to me. I didn't work or sacrifice for what I think I want.

Create in me a clean heart and renew in me the right spirit (Psalms 51:10)

When I feel envy, instead of causing harm to myself or my brother/sister, I will choose inspiration over envy and remember that I am accepted in the beloved (Ephesians 1:6) In Jesus Name. Amen.

Music is Medicine

From Wanda's Playlist:

Destiny – Tina Campbell

Great is Thy Faithfulness – Melvin Crispell III

Find Your Song

....

....

As you continue healing from Crab Mentality Disease, you will start experiencing joy and contentment and a sense of personal satisfaction.

My Healing Journey

1. What does jealousy mean to you?

2. Why do you need to heal from jealousy?

3. What do you need to do to stop being jealous?

4. If nothing changes, what will that cost you?

5. What sort of environment do you need to set up to be successful?

Scripture

And now, dear brothers and sisters, one final thing. Fix your thoughts on what is true, and honorable, and right, and pure, and lovely, and admirable. Think about things that are excellent and worthy of praise. Philippians 4:8 NLT.

Prayer

God, thank you for teaching me how dangerous being jealous is. According to your word, peace of mind makes the body healthy, but jealousy is like a cancer. (Proverbs 14:30). I repent for being jealous and renounce how I act when I am jealous.

I arrest the spirit of jealousy in my heart, remove it from me along with greed, laziness, pride. Open my heart, mind and eyes so I can see when I am acting like a crab.

In the name of Jesus, I break and take authority over all these behaviors so that I can honestly celebrate with other people. I'm tired of being controlled by jealousy that is making me sick. Teach me how to be content with what I have (Philippians 4:11) and not be jealous of family members, friends or people I know.

Give me the courage to change my thinking and behaviors. I will stop this disease from being passed down to my children. In Jesus Name, Amen.

Music is Medicine

From Wanda's Playlist:

Humility (A song of Repentance) Malkah Norwood

Thristy – Marvin Sapp

Find Your Song

I CHOOSE TO HEAL!

CHAPTER 4

COMPARISON AND COMPETITION

Don't be insecure when you see someone is rising in his/her career or life, in general. Be inspired by what they accomplished. Don't pull them down. Here's a wonderful suggestion: ask them how they achieve things and learn from them. Avoid Crab Mentality
— Venchito Tampon

Once someone is infected with the Crab Mentality Virus, they will always compare themselves to others and view everything and everyone as a competition.

Competition – trying to compete in everything to prove to themselves and others that they are "better."

Overly Competition — as defined in the Urban Dictionary — is someone that is a big pain because they turn everything into a competition. Their primary goal is to steal attention for themselves. If it is not about them, they will downplay its importance. Secret and behind-the-back moves are common, two-faced.

This is how, by comparing ourselves, we cause harm to ourselves and the people we are connected to.

There is a big difference between healthy competition and comparison.

Healthy competition is good. It can motivate you to be the best you can be. Comparison, on the other hand, is not good. It makes us feel bad about ourselves from the start.

Here are some ways we hurt ourselves and other people by comparing and competing.

1. We don't celebrate our wins when we compare ourselves to others.

2. We end up resenting family, friends and others when we compare ourselves to them.

3. We may experience depression and lower self-esteem by comparing ourselves to others.

4. We fall in love with fantasy instead of reality when we compare ourselves to others.

5. Results in a pyrrhic victory, a victory that comes at a substantial cost, making the cost to win not worth it.

10 Ways 2 Stop Comparing Yourself

1. Practice Gratitude.

2. Learn to be Contented.

3. Don't compare your life to the life your family or friends show in public.

4. Focus on your strengths, what you are good at.

5. Reject FOMO (Fear Of Missing Out).

6. Learn to compete with yourself instead of others.

7. Spend less time on social media.

8. Retrain your mind by stopping negative talk.

9. Involve yourself in healthy competition and reject comparison.

10. Focus on your goals – spiritual, lifestyle, family.

My Healing Journey

1. Why is everything a competition to you?

2. What impact is it having on you?

3. What really MATTERS?

4. If nothing changes, what will that cost you?

5. What do I have the power to do right now?

Scripture

I praise you because of the wonderful way you created me. Everything you do is marvelous! Of this I have no doubt. Psalms 139:14 (CEV)

Prayer

God, I praise you because of who you are. Thank you for leading me in the way I should go. I look to you for guidance and direction. The plans that you have for me are to prosper me, not to harm me, plans to give me hope and a future (Jeremiah 29:11). Father, forgive me for focusing on other people's lives when you have a specific plan and purpose for me. I will not compare myself with other people as if one is better and another worse. I have better things to do with my time and my life. Teach me a more excellent way. In Jesus Name, Amen.

Music is Medicine

From Wanda's Playlist:

You know my Name – Tasha Cobb Leonard

Thank you – Benita Washington

Manifest – Jonathan Nelson

Find Your Song

Keep Healing!

CHAPTER 5

DO I HAVE CRAB MENTALITY DISEASE?

You will know the truth and the truth will set you free.
John 8:32 (CEV)

The first step in identifying if you have The Crab Mentality Virus, which without intervention will develop into Crab Mentality Disease, is by self-assessment; recognizing that you are behaving like a crab in the bucket.

Crab Mentality Disease Quiz

11. Do you feel happy when something bad happens to people you know?

      Yes   No

12. Do you make negative comments about a person's success?

Yes   No

13. Do you feel like someone is a threat when they are growing and achieving their goals?

Yes   No

14. Is your family full of secrets?

Yes   No

15. Are you a people pleaser (a go along to get along) type of person?

Yes   No

16. Have you said or have you heard that a family member "thinks they're better than us."?

Yes   No

17. Is it hard for you to celebrate with other people?

Yes   No

18. Are you a jealous person?

Yes   No

19. In your family culture, is verbal abuse (gossiping, name calling and so called "jokes") acceptable communication?

Yes   No

20. Have you said or have you heard that a family member "forgot where they came from"?

Yes   No

If you score high on the quiz with 7 or more yes answers, you most likely have CMD. The first thing you should do is admit that you have it. Then identify the underlying issues that are causing you to be infected and affected with Crab Mentality Disease.

What You Can Do Right Now?

Replace your thinking, instead of focusing on what others are doing and achieving, with focusing on you, your own goals and becoming a better you.

Look for the positive aspects of other people's accomplishments. For instance, if you see someone achieve something that you want to achieve, instead of being jealous and then trying to diminish their accomplishment, try to see the lessons you can learn from them and apply it to your own journey.

Remember, to avoid Crab Mentality Virus you must first recognize that it is your issue that you can change, if you want to!

Start with the underlying issues that's causing you to act like a crab in the bucket and pray about changing your mindset. Change your outlook on someone's success. When someone in the family wins, the whole family wins.

My Healing Journey

1. How is acting like a crab working for you?

2. Are you mad at others or yourself?

3. What is the risk if you change?

4. What is the risk if you don't change?

5. Who is in control, who decides?

Scripture

"The heart is deceitful above all things, and it is extremely sick; Who can understand it fully and know its secret motives?" Jeremiah 17:9 (AMP)

Prayer

Father, thank you for revealing to me the condition of my heart and mind. I repent. Please create a clean heart in me. God put a new and loyal spirit in me (Psalms 51:10). Heal my broken heart. Heal my damaged emotions. My desire is for me and my family to be blessed, so I will not follow the advice of the wicked or follow in their steps. I trust you, sharpen my discernment, yes wisdom is the main thing. I claim healing and restoration in my family bloodline. Re-establish your purpose in our lives so we may follow in your will while teaching our future generations to do the same.

Thank you for forgiveness, grace, and compassion. In Jesus Name, Amen.

Music Is Medicine

From Wanda's Playlist:

Lord Deliver Me - LeAndria Johnson &
Donald Lawrence

Another Place – Micah Stampley

Find Your Song

Healing Is For Me!

CHAPTER 6

THE GREAT ESCAPE

Don't let anyone deceive you. Associating with bad people will ruin decent people. 1 Corinthians 15:33 (GNT)

How to tell if someone is infected with the Crab Mentality Virus

It is helpful to identify whether someone has Crab Mentality. The number one symptom of CMV is someone who will often discourage or sabotage others. Here are some other signs and symptoms that someone might have CMV include:

1. The tendency to speak negatively about others.

2. The tendency to automatically react negatively to the accomplishments of other people.

3. The habit of taking part in the accomplishments of someone else in to diminish them by sabotage

4. The habit of viewing the accomplishments of others as reflecting negatively on oneself.

5. The habit of viewing others as being in direct competition, even when that is not the case.

6. Expression of satisfaction towards other people's misfortune.

7. Lack of compassion toward others.

8. An inability to work well with others.

9. The habit of complaining and criticizing continually without attempting to solve the problem.

10. INSECURITY AND BITTERNESS toward one's own abilities, accomplishments, or status. However, some people may display the opposite behavior, inflating their own abilities, accomplishments or status to diminish those of others.

If You Are the Target, the opposition can be either verbal, physical, emotional, spiritual or a combination. Here is a short list of some scheme(s) utilized:

Monitoring - observing and checking the target to obtain information and to determine the effectiveness of the attack.

Gang stalking — when the crabs left in the barrel group attack the crab that is either attempting to get out, is out or stay out. The gang is used to co-sign (justify) and cover-up crab like behaviors.

Collateral Damage — accidental harm, and damage to people connected to the crab that is out of the bucket.

Frenemy — a person who pretends to be a friend to obtain information

Craftiness — a person highly skilled in trickery, manipulation and deception

Devalue—reduce or underestimate the worth or importance of dreams and goals that are opposite of the family or group culture.

Sadly, the Family Member who heals from the virus would be seen as an outcast or traitor since they are attempting to break the mindset and behavior pattern of The Crab Mentality Disease in the family bloodline

In addition to addressing Crab Mentality in ourselves, we are confronted with Crab Mentality in others. The first step in dealing with Crab Mentality is to acknowledge and accept that they carry CMV in them. When you do this, ensure you understand how CMV influences them regarding their thoughts, statements, and actions. If possible, try to understand what is causing them to have CMV in the first place.

Then there are several things that you can do in response to their behaviors. Although we understand we cannot change anyone but ourselves, we can utilize the same methods we would use to avoid being infected with Crab Mentality Virus, known as infection prevention. We also make sure that we interact with others with behaviors that are anti-Crab Mentality.

You Need Boundaries!

Learning to set boundaries is an important part of maintaining our physical and emotional health.

Boundaries are guidelines or personal laws we establish for ourselves in any relationship to prevent us from hurting ourselves or others.

Setting healthy boundaries is necessary for self-care. Where there are no boundaries, we may end up feeling used, fearful, and disrespected.

5 Types of Boundaries

1. Physical Boundaries

2. Thoughts and Ideas Boundaries

3. Emotional Boundaries

4. Material Boundaries

5. Time Boundaries

Always remember, you can't change someone who does not want to change, a person who is infected/affected with The Crab Mentality Disease is sick. Instead, focus on your mindset and how you respond by doing that. It lessens the impact that their Crab Mentality will have on you. Here are some suggested boundaries:

1. Ignore Them

2. Realize that their Crab Mentality is driven mostly by their own issues, rather than by anything that you did, even if you are a target of their behavior.

3. Accept that someone's Crab Mentality is their issue, don't make it your issue by trying to solve it.

4. Forgive them for acting like a crab, they are sick forgiveness is the best thing you can do for everyone.

5. Stay focus move forward in your dreams, goals, and assignment rather than on other people's negativity.

6. Refuse to clap back/retaliate by engaging in Crab Mentality behaviors; decide to do the opposite.

In some cases, the best long-term solution is to simply distance yourself from people who are infected with the Crab Mentality Virus

Be ok with giving the gift of your low or no contact to people who do not appreciate or respect you.

Always remember, you can use some of the same interventions to avoid being infected and affected with Crab Mentality Disease. Stay watchful on your mindset, feelings and actions. Crab Mentality Virus is transmitted by their own internal emotional issues: fear, jealousy, envy, and insecurity and not by anything you did.

My Healing Journey

1. What can you learn from your past?

2. What do I want my legacy to be?

3. What would you do if you were not afraid?

4. If nothing changes, what would be the cost to you?

5. What is the best use of your time RIGHT NOW?

Scripture

Beloved, I pray that in every way you may succeed and prosper and be in good health [physically], just as [I know] your soul prospers [spiritually]. 3 John 1:2 (AMP)

Prayer

Thank you, Father, that I can come to you when I have problems problems. I will not worry about the wicked or envy those who do wrong (Psalms 37:1) I will continue to focus on healing so I can stop bleeding on people who didn't cut me. I will not become bitter, I will become better. I will learn the lesson and use them for good. I am not ashamed. I am not a victim, I am more than a conqueror. I do not have the power to change my loved ones, but you do because you are the bondage breaker. As I pray for them, show me how to be wise as a serpent and harmless as a dove (Matthew 10:16) I need you to give me the courage and strength to set boundaries with persons infected and affected with Crab Mentality Disease. I will forgive myself. I will forgive them and bless them. In the name of Jesus, Amen

Music is Medicine

From Wanda's Playlist:

Your Tears Have Paid Off

Vashawn Mitchell & Monique Walker

Find My Peace – Naomi Raine

Find Your Song

....

....

DON'T GIVE UP!

CHAPTER 7

I GOT THE VICTORY

I'm free indeed
in Christ I'm free indeed
no chains holding me
it's who I choose to be — Timothy Readick

Now that the Crab Mentality Disease has been arrested, how do you keep from being infected and affected again?

Remember that Crab Mentality Disease is chronic disease spiritually, mentally and physically. It may be a lifelong battle. It can come back to make trouble (like a roaring lion). When old thoughts, feelings and temptations recur, immediately rebuke and refuse them. We have heard the saying, "hurt people, hurt people." This is a painful disease. Below are signs of emotional pain. Please, don't ignore them.

Signs of Emotional Pain

- Anger
- Mood Swings
- Insomnia
- Poor Self-Esteem
- Holding On To The Grudges
- Difficulty In Forgiving Others
- Lack Of Social Communication

Pray that God will send people to help and protect you. There is nothing wrong with getting professional help on your journey to wholeness. Faith without work is dead. You must do the work. Ask God to show you who you really are: the good, the bad the ugly the mask has to go. Do not be afraid to change.

Keep a sharp eye on your thoughts and feelings to ensure that they are healthy. Pray for and continue to develop discernment so that you will be alert, sober and vigilant. Wake up and Stay Woke against Crab Mentality Disease.

Walk in forgiveness as a lifestyle. Forgive quickly. Ongoing forgiveness is very important. Watch your thoughts and feelings toward others, especially if there is a history of trouble in the relationship. I know it's hard, but forgiveness is the only way to stop the spread of this deadly disease.

When you mess up, repent quickly and close the door fast. As soon as you realize that you have been returning to crab-like behaviors, repent, renounce and change whatever thoughts and behaviors that are involved.

Don't forget that self-care is important. In addition to using boundaries, ensure you get adequate rest, exercise, a healthy diet and any other activities that'd help you manage stress if it does not trigger harmful behavior to yourself or others.

My Healing Journey

1. How will I know when I have the Victory?

2. What can you learn from your past?

3. What will you do differently this time?

4. What sort of environment do you need to set up to succeed?

5. What do I want my legacy to be?

Scripture

Brothers and sisters, if someone is overtaken in any wrongdoing, you who are spiritual, restore such a person with a gentle spirit, watching out for yourselves so that you also won't be tempted. Galatians 6:1 CSB.

Prayer

Father, I just want to say Thank You. Thank you for being the Healer. Your word says that I can ask for anything in your name and you will do it (John 14:14). In the name of Jesus, heal me, make me whole in mind, body, and spirit. I have the Faith. Now I have to do something. I have to decide to change and be intentional about changing. I take authority over the Crab Mentality Virus and Crab Mentality Disease. Please order my steps so I can do what is required in the spiritual and natural. What is not transformed is transferred. From generation to generation, I'm ending it NOW! We praise you; we honor you for the victory. In Jesus Name, amen.

Music is Medicine

From Wanda's Playlist:

Overcomer - Eddie James

I Made It Out Alright – John P Kee

I Got the Victory – Ricky Dillard

Find Your Song

PASS YOUR HEALING ON!

About The Author

Wanda Currie is a Life Coach and the Founder of Vision of Recovery, which believes in and practices a Christ-centered approach to Mental Health Care. Wanda is a Christian Counselor & Certified Life Coach. She also has a Master's Degree in Social Work from Howard University.

Vision of Recovery specializes in addiction and trauma recovery by integrating biblically based resources with coaching and counseling interventions to treat the whole person: Spiritually, Emotionally, and Physically.

Wanda writes a monthly blog and is the host of a weekly podcast "Surviving Your Pain."

To contact the Author and to learn more about Vision of Recovery services, please visit www.visionofrecovery.com